Dear Parent:

Congratulations! Your child is taking the first steps on an exciting journey. The destination? Independent reading!

STEP INTO READING® will help your child get there. The program offers five steps to reading success. Each step includes fun stories and colorful art. There are also Step into Reading Sticker Books, Step into Reading Math Readers, Step into Reading Write-In Readers, Step into Reading Phonics Readers, and Step into Reading Phonics First Steps! Boxed Sets—a complete literacy program with something for every child.

Learning to Read, Step by Step!

Ready to Read   Preschool–Kindergarten
• big type and easy words • rhyme and rhythm • picture clues
For children who know the alphabet and are eager to begin reading.

Reading with Help   Preschool–Grade 1
• basic vocabulary • short sentences • simple stories
For children who recognize familiar words and sound out new words with help.

Reading on Your Own   Grades 1–3
• engaging characters • easy-to-follow plots • popular topics
For children who are ready to read on their own.

Reading Paragraphs   Grades 2–3
• challenging vocabulary • short paragraphs • exciting stories
For newly independent readers who read simple sentences with confidence.

Ready for Chapters   Grades 2–4
• chapters • longer paragraphs • full-color art
For children who want to take the plunge into chapter books but still like colorful pictures.

STEP INTO READING® is designed to give every child a successful reading experience. The grade levels are only guides. Children can progress through the steps at their own speed, developing confidence in their reading, no matter what their grade.

Remember, a lifetime love of reading starts with a single step!

*Dedicated to the great state of Wyoming and all its
citizens, living and extinct. —R.T.B.*

*The author and editor would like to thank
Dr. Philip Currie and Dr. Thomas R. Holtz, Jr.,
for their assistance in the preparation of this book.*

Text copyright © 2003 by Dr. Robert T. Bakker.
Illustrations copyright © 2003 by Michael Skrepnick.
All rights reserved under International and Pan-American Copyright Conventions. Published
in the United States by Random House Children's Books, a division of Random House, Inc.,
New York, and simultaneously in Canada by Random House of Canada Limited, Toronto.

www.stepintoreading.com

Educators and librarians, for a variety of teaching tools, visit us at
www.randomhouse.com/teachers

Library of Congress Cataloging-in-Publication Data
Bakker, Robert T.
Raptor pack / by Dr. Robert T. Bakker ; illustrated by Michael Skrepnick.
    p. cm. — (Step into reading. A step 5 book)
SUMMARY: A paleontologist discusses what is known of the physical characteristics and behavior
of *Deinonychus,* a member of the raptor family of dinosaurs.
ISBN 0-375-82303-4 (trade) — ISBN 0-375-92303-9 (lib. bdg.)
1. Deinonychus—Montana—Juvenile literature. [1. Deinonychus. 2. Dinosaurs.]
I. Skrepnick, Michael William, ill. II. Title. III. Series: Step into reading. Step 5 book.
QE862.S3 B35 2003
567.912—dc21
2002017946

Printed in the United States of America
First Edition   10 9 8 7 6

Raptor Pack

by Dr. Robert T. Bakker

illustrated by Michael Skrepnick

Random House 🏠 New York

Introduction

My name is Bob Bakker and I'm a paleontologist. My job is to dig up fossil bones and figure out how dinosaurs lived. I think it's the best job in the universe.

I'm going to tell you a story about a pack of raptors. Then I'm going to tell you how we figured out that the story is mostly true.

Chapter One

Imagine a summer morning 120 million years ago in what is now Montana. Huge, scaly monsters move in herds over a dry lake bed. They're dinosaurs; three kinds of giant plant-eaters. The sound of leaves being munched fills the air. There's an undercurrent of grunts and snorts and wheezes and hisses. Giant veggie-saurs bump into each other as they compete for the juiciest green morsels. Each herbivore's tummy emits rumbling sounds—the noise of contented digestion. There's a smell of crushed fruit.

The land is flat and low and dry. It's hot all year round. The trees are mostly evergreens with thick green needles. The only plants with flowers are some small shrubs. The dinosaur herds kick up clouds of red dust as they walk along.

Towering over everybody else are a dozen gigantic brachiosaurs (BRACK-ee-o-SAWRS). They're long-necked dinosaurs who reach forty feet up to feed on the tops of trees. You see a family of ankylosaurs (ANG-ki-lo-SAWRS), too. These armor-plated dinosaurs are as big as elephants, with spikes on their shoulders. They're munching on plants low to the ground.

Beyond the lake bed is a riverbank, where trees grow close together. There you see dozens and dozens of moose-sized plant-eaters. They have square heads and *really* long tails. These are tenontosaurs (te-NON-to-SAWRS), and they're the favorite prey of dinosaurs called raptors.

Suddenly, the brachiosaurs and ankylosaurs stop eating. They smell something in the wind. Something that scares them. A brachiosaur points its nose toward the trees. It snorts so loud that the tree trunks shake. Leaves fall to the ground. The ankylosaurs hiss and grumble and stomp their feet. They're angry, too. They *hate* that smell.

But the long-tailed tenontosaurs can't smell any danger. Their nostrils are stuffed up with dust and dirt. And the wind is blowing in the wrong direction. But one old tenontosaur sees two shapes stepping quickly through the trees. Two other shapes move slowly in the tall ferns on the other side of the herd. The old plant-eater has many memories of shapes like these. *Bad* memories. He screams.

Ten other tenontosaurs start to scream, too. All the veggie-saur brains switch to stampede mode.

The whole herd starts running. The oldest members kick and bump into each other. The youngsters try to keep out of the way. It's dangerous to be in the middle of a dino-stampede.

Hidden in the trees and ferns, four raptors watch the scene with great care. That's because they *too* have memories. They remember how big, healthy tenontosaurs are dangerous and defend themselves with sharp beaks and claws. All four raptors have scars on their faces and legs from attacks they've made in the last two years.

But one tenontosaur catches the raptors' attention. It's limping. The raptors rush in from both sides, dodging the snapping beaks of the healthy plant-eaters. They leap up to see their target. One raptor jumps up and swings its back feet at the tenontosaur. The raptor's sharp hind claws cut deep into its thigh. The tenontosaur trips and falls. In seconds, all four raptors stand on its body.

After the kill, the raptors pant hard.
Once they catch their breath, they make a
drumming sound inside their chests. It's a
signal. It means "Come and get it!" Seven
little raptor chicks the size of chickens
scamper out of their hiding places. The
air is full of gulping and swallowing and
grunting noises.

An hour later, the raptors have tummies stuffed full of meat. They lick dried blood and flesh from the feathery scales that cover their bodies. By noon the sun is blazing. They look for a way to escape the hot ground. A tall, thick tree stands nearby. They go to it.

The adult raptors reach up with their long arms and begin to climb. Using the hooked claws on their hands and feet, they pull themselves onto the lower branches. The chicks zip up the tree in seconds. Within minutes, the whole pack is asleep.

Snores and belches come from the tree all night. Just before dawn, a dark mass sneaks around the tree trunk. It's an acrocanthosaur (ak-ro-KAN-tho-SAWR)— a giant predator, or meat-eater. He has jaws so big he can swallow a raptor whole. And he'd like to, too. The big guy hisses and looks up into the trees. He thumps the bark with his snout.

"BLECH!" One raptor chick upchucks a mouthful of toe bone. The big predator gets hit on the head.

"BLECH! BLECH! BLECH!" One good upchuck leads to another. All the chicks hurl bone bits at the predator below. The 5,000-pound meat-eater growls, but can't climb. He can't get at the pack. He snorts one last time and walks away.

Chapter Two

So . . . how do scientists *know* that raptors really did things like this? We know because we've dug up their bones and the bones of their prey. We've mapped the places where they lived, locating the mountains, lakes, and rivers. We've found the fossilized roots of plants that grew back then, so we can figure out what the landscape looked like. And we can look at living predators, such as leopards and hyenas, to see how they live their lives.

Hundreds of scientists have helped us understand the raptors. Plus, we have volunteers who help us dig. All these discoveries were used to bring raptors back to life in the *Jurassic Park* movies.

The first fossil raptor pack was dug in 1964 near Bridger, Montana. I was there as part of the team that dug the bones for Yale professor John H. Ostrom. We knew we were digging up some kind of new dinosaur. The claws were weird—much sharper than any we'd seen before. Ordinary dino-predators had hand claws shaped like an eagle's. They were thick and rounded on the bottom. They worked like a meat hook.

Meat-hook claws are good for grabbing prey and holding on. But this new dinosaur had hand-claw bones that were narrow and super sharp on the bottom. They were more like a curved knife than a hook.

Professor Ostrom gave this bizarre new dinosaur the name *Deinonychus* (die-NON-ih-kus), or "terrible claw." It was a member of the famous raptor family, and a very close relative of *Velociraptor* (vuh-LAHS-uh-RAP-tur), dug in Mongolia.

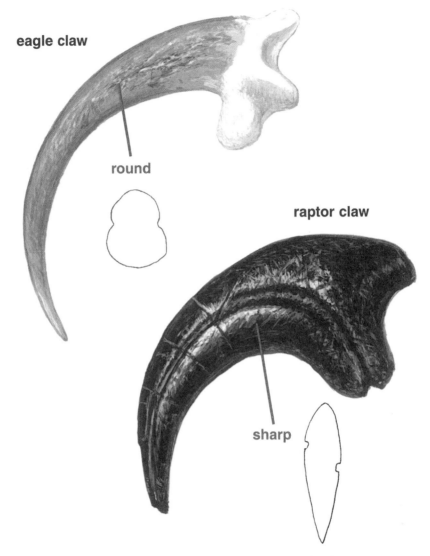

eagle claw

round

raptor claw

sharp

All raptors are built a lot like birds. Specimens dug from special lake beds in China show that their bodies had a complete coat of downlike feathers.

In our Montana dig, bones from four raptors were all mixed up together. My first job as a student paleontologist was to sit in the lab and sort out what knee went with what shin. Then I drew a picture of what *Deinonychus* looked like when it was alive. Next, we wanted to figure out how this body worked.

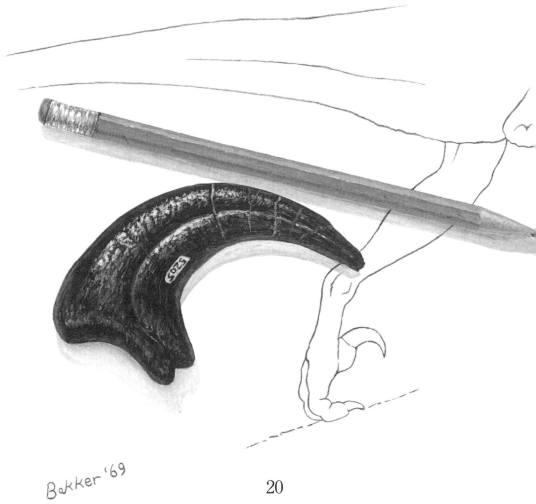

Bakker '69

Chapter Three

The first puzzling thing about *Deinonychus* was its size—it was a lightweight. Most famous dino-predators were big guys. *T. rex,* the giant meat-eater who lived after *Deinonychus,* grew to weigh 12,000 pounds. But even a *big* adult *Deinonychus* would only weigh around 150 pounds! Small size didn't make sense.

Meat-eaters eat plant-eaters (or "veggie-saurs," as I call them). Today, most 150-pound meat-eaters kill prey about the same size as they are. But in the layer of rock where we dug *Deinonychus,* we found veggie-saurs weighing up to 100,000 pounds!

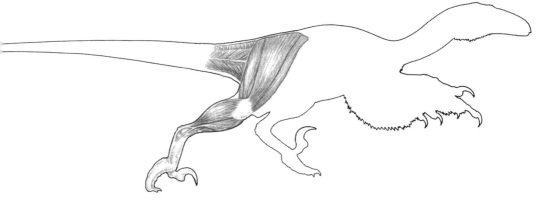

We found hardly *any* veggie-saurs as small as 500 pounds. There were some turtles and rare turkey-sized dinosaurs, but not enough to feed a raptor. So it looked like *Deinonychus* had to kill things much bigger than itself. But how?

It couldn't kill big things by biting them. *Deinonychus* had sharp, curved teeth with saw edges, but they were tiny teeth. They were good for cutting meat off a dead body, but not big enough to kill a large dinosaur. And its skull bones were too thin to deliver a hard bite. So how did *Deinonychus* take down big prey?

The puzzle was finally solved when we realized that *Deinonychus* was a kick-boxer. We were looking at the wrong end of the raptor. The killing apparatus was in the rear. The strongest parts of its body were its hind legs. Marks on the bones showed us where the leg muscles attached, and the muscles for kicking backward were especially strong—ten times more powerful than the jaw muscles. *Deinonychus* could kick backward much, *much* harder than it could bite! If it had a deadly weapon on its hind foot, *Deinonychus* would be very dangerous.

Guess what?

That's exactly what *Deinonychus* had! Its most deadly weapons were its hind claws. There was one fighting claw on each foot, shaped like the hand claws—only bigger. A *Deinonychus*'s hind leg could slice open a veggie-saur in one stroke.

If *Deinonychus* was a kick-boxer, then it should have been built for jumping and dodging. Ostrom showed that it was. The raptor was so light, and its hind legs so strong, it could jump higher than a basketball player! And it could turn in midair.

Deinonychus had a two-part tail. The part near the body had muscles and joints for quick movement. But the rear part was long and light with hardly any muscle at all. It was like the long pole acrobats use to balance on a high wire. All around the rear tailbones were bony rods as thin as fishing line.

These lines were connected to the muscles. When the tail muscles pulled, the rear tail could flip around so the raptor could turn in midair. There's nothing alive today with a quick-flip tail like a raptor's.

Chapter Four

Deinonychus had to do more than kill prey. It had to survive in a tough environment. Dying from thirst was a real threat. The only big fish fossils we find near our raptors are from lungfish—and lungfish today survive by breathing air when rivers dry up completely.

In the rocks where we dug these raptors, we also found fossil lake beds. These lake beds had minerals in them that grow only in salt lakes. Salt lakes form when summers are so hot and dry that a lot of water evaporates into the air. This makes the water left behind too salty to drink.

Deinonychus could get water from the blood of its prey, but how could the raptors escape the heat? On dry lake beds in modern Africa, leopards climb up into trees to get away from the searing heat at ground level and to enjoy cool breezes. Could *Deinonychus* climb?

Most meat-eating dinosaurs couldn't. Their arms weren't long enough. Famous predators like *Tyrannosaurus rex* and *Allosaurus* (AL-o-SAWR-us) had arms so short that their fingers couldn't reach their ears! Raptors, though, were very different. *Deinonychus* had very long arms and fingers. Its shoulder joints were different, too.

In "normal" meat-eaters like *T. rex* and *Allosaurus,* the shoulder joint was tight and wouldn't let the arm move up much. But raptors had a much looser shoulder joint. They could spread their arms sideways to grab. *Deinonychus* was able to reach out and pull itself up into a tree with its fingers and toes. And it was strong enough to haul up prey parts, too.

Climbing can be a lifesaver for another reason—to avoid bigger predators. In the same area where we dug our raptor pack, we found the bones of a rare, giant predator called an acrocanthosaur. It was twenty times heavier than *Deinonychus.* This guy could easily steal a raptor's kill from off the ground—and gobble up a few raptors while he was at it! *Deinonychus* could use the curved claws on its hands and feet to get *into* the trees and *out of* the danger.

acrocanthosaur—the giant enemy

One *Deinonychus* hunting by itself was a dangerous predator. Still, it could find itself in serious trouble. Fossil footprints show us that most veggie-saurs traveled in big herds. Herd animals can counterattack. Today, water buffalo herds will sometimes stomp an attacking tiger to death. But lions are group hunters, and four lions attacking together can bring down a water buffalo.

Did Deinonychus hunt in packs? Fossil footprints would tell us, but we haven't found any raptor footprints yet. We *do* have another clue, however.

When we dug our first *Deinonychus* bones in 1964, we found three or four adult skeletons in one small spot. They had been buried by a flood. They could have drowned, or they could have died of disease just before the flood. But one thing was certain: these meat-eaters were together before they died. *But why?*

Chapter Five

Predators don't usually hang out in groups if they don't hunt together. Tigers are like this—they mostly hunt alone, and you don't see bunches of tigers lying around together. But lions are social predators. They hunt and raise their young and sleep and snore together.

Those three or four adult *Deinonychus* we dug were probably a pack, a group from one species who hunted together.

So what was the pack hunting? Scientists can figure that out by using what I call "Dinosaur Crime-Scene Investigation." It's a new technique that lets us go back in time and follow dinosaurian meat-eaters. Just as detectives look at bullets found at crime scenes to identify the gun that shot them, we look for dinosaur "bullets" among the fossilized remains of prey animals to identify the predators that chewed on them. These dino-bullets are teeth that predators lost while feeding on prey. Losing teeth didn't hurt the dinosaurs. New teeth grew in their jaws as long as they lived.

Humans grow two sets of teeth—baby teeth and adult teeth. If you break an adult tooth, you won't grow a new one. But raptors never ran out of teeth. When one fell out, another was there to replace it. Sharks and crocodiles grow teeth this way, and so do most lizards.

If you X-ray the jaws of a meat-eating dinosaur, you'll see a few teeth stacked on top of each other in each tooth socket. New teeth start growing at the bottom of the stack, and the whole stack is always moving up.

X-ray of raptor snout

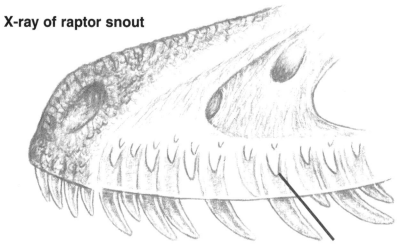

new teeth growing in socket

adult bullet   baby bullet

Before the top tooth fell out, chemicals in the dinosaur's body dissolved the root—the part that held it inside the socket. Usually the top tooth fell out when the animal was eating. So a tooth without a root is a dino-bullet that was lost during the "crime" of . . . eating.

Police detectives study bullets under the microscope to identify the guns that shot them. The size of the bullet, the marks on its side, and the sharpness of the point are all clues. Dinosaur teeth give clues, too—if you look carefully. When we put tooth-bullets under the scope, we can tell what kind of dinosaur "fired" them. Raptor teeth are sharp with a coarse saw edge on the rear. Other kinds of meat-eaters have thicker and blunter teeth, better for crushing.

Dinosaur detectives have to be careful when they find a fossil tooth that has its root attached. That's not a bullet. It's part of a dinosaur who was killed by predators or drought or disease. Roots hold a tooth tightly in the socket. A dinosaur had to die and rot before a tooth with its root in place could fall out.

Crocodiles alive today leave tooth-bullets at "crime scenes" like dinosaurs did. Sometimes, in Australia, a saltwater croc will attack a surfer. Afterward you can find rootless croc teeth stuck in the surfboard. (Sometimes in the surfer, too.)

We wanted to find spots where raptors fed and left their tooth-bullets. Plus—we wanted to find spots where they *didn't* feed.

A big meat-eater has the toughest job in Nature. *Why?* Your lunch can fight back. Big, strong vegetarians will charge as soon as they catch a meat-eater's scent. And some herbivores have special anti-predator weapons. Rhinos today use their horns to spear lions. And giant armadillos have armor so tough that jaguars can't bite through it.

Where did we find *Deinonychus* bullets? Modern hyenas try to avoid elephants and hippos. So we figured *Deinonychus* would try to avoid *really* dangerous veggie-saurs like brachiosaurs. These gigantic plant-eaters were so heavy, they could squash a *Deinonychus* with one step. And the pack was not likely to take on any ankylosaurs, either. Even the strongest *Deinonychus* kick would bounce off an ankylosaur's armor.

Our hunches worked out. We didn't find any *Deinonychus* bullets in the one spot we found that was full of brachiosaur and ankylosaur fossils.

Okay. So if *Deinonychus* avoided strong, dangerous veggie-saurs, what was its favorite prey? We figured it should be the most common midsize plant-eaters who didn't have armor. That's the way things usually work in Nature. On the African plains today, hyenas are the most common predators, and they tend to eat zebra and wildebeest, the most common midsize plant-eaters.

So who was the most common midsize veggie-saur in *Deinonychus*'s habitat? The square-jawed, about-1,200-pound *Tenontosaurus*. We found dozens and dozens of these guys scattered over a hundred square miles. And that's where we found our *Deinonychus* bullets—right smack with the tenontosaurs!

Were raptors ever . . . cannibals? That's not a disgusting thought. Being a cannibal makes sense for most predators. Most wild meat-eaters are always hungry and short of food. If one of your own kind dies, why not eat him or her? It's Nature's recycling. *So . . . did <u>Deinonychus</u> ever eat its own kind?*

Yes! In one spot in Wyoming, we dug up a raptor that had been chewed to bits. All that was left were finger and tailbones. There were tooth-bullets at the crime scene. Whose bullets? You guessed it. A raptor very much like *Deinonychus.*

Did Deinonychus poop? Well, of course! Everybody's got to. Sometimes we see fossil veggie-saur droppings, but feces from meateating dinos are rare. *How come?*

Think about it. *Deinonychus* was built like a big bird. What comes out of the rear end of an eagle? Eagle droppings! Liquid feces. When eagle poop hits the ground, it splats. The fecal matter isn't firm and can't fossilize because it doesn't have enough bone minerals in it. But hyena poop and dog poop are full of bone bits and make excellent fossils.

owl pellet

So why doesn't eagle poop have much bone in it? That's because when an eagle eats a rabbit, most of its bones don't come out the eagle's rear. They come out the eagle's mouth! Hawks and eagles and owls throw up the bones of their prey after the meat has been digested. If you find a tree where an owl is living, you'll find a pile of "owl pellets" on the ground. These are wads of bones and fur from mice and shrews eaten by the bird.

Unlike wolves, *Deinonychus* probably upchucked more bones than it pooped. So we look for "dino-pellets"—fossilized wads of prey bones. And we find them. At one spot in 1999, my crew dug up a mass of broken ribs and backbones. And right with the bone wad was a dinosaur bullet—the rootless tooth of a meat-eating predator. That tooth probably came from the same dinosaur who upchucked the bones.

Was <u>Deinonychus</u> a good parent? If you hatched out of a *Deinonychus* egg 120 million years ago, would you find yourself alone? That's the way most lizards hatch. If you're a baby Komodo dragon lizard, your parents aren't around to help, so you must find your first meal by yourself. But eagle parents *are* around when their chicks hatch. And they feed the chicks at the nest until they're fully grown.

So what was dino-predator family life like? Lizard or eagle?

We've got a lot of evidence from one special spot in Wyoming, called Nail Quarry. A dinosaur predator we nicknamed "Wyoming-raptor" (a distant relative of *Deinonychus*) left a wonderful crime scene full of dino-bullets. We found a hundred teeth without roots in this spot, and every one of them came from the same kind of predator. And chewed-up veggie-saur bones were piled in with the bullets.

"Wyoming-raptor" had spent months, maybe even years, dragging in prey bodies and eating them. *Did these parent predators take care of the youngsters? And did the whole family eat together? How could we find out?*

Easy. If the chicks ate with their parents, then the chicks must have lost teeth in the same place where the adults lost theirs. We should find baby bullets mixed in with the adult bullets.

And that's exactly what we *did* find! Right next to the adult "Wyoming-raptor" bullets, we found tiny baby bullets from predators who had just hatched. The adult teeth were twelve times bigger than the baby teeth, but they had the exact same shape under the microscope. All these "Wyoming-raptors"—adults *and* chicks— were eating at this spot at the same time. This dinosaur family stayed together because it preyed together.

Baby alligators chase small fry like bugs and crayfish because the gator mom doesn't hunt for her babies. But eagle hatchlings eat big prey—often bigger than themselves! That's because the mom and dad eagle bring food to their chicks. So how about our dinosaur predator? Did its chicks have to hunt their own food?

Nope. All the baby bullets we found were next to gigantic prey bones. These babies were gnawing on bodies that were 100,000 times as big as themselves. That's

like you sitting at the dinner table and
eating an elephant. The only way these
babies could get such a big chunk of food
was if their parents brought it in.

And so we concluded that the adults
were doing the hunting, and fed their chicks
just like eagles do. "Wyoming-raptor" lived a
little earlier than *Deinonychus* and wasn't
quite so birdlike. We figure *Deinonychus* was
even more like an eagle in the way it raised
its chicks.

Deinonychus and the other raptors are some of my favorite dinosaurs. They were fast and deadly, graceful and smart. And they managed to survive for seventy million years in a harsh environment.

Sometimes, when I'm eating lunch at a dinosaur quarry full of tooth-bullets, I lean back on the cliff and look all around. I wish I had a time machine so I could visit the raptors when they were alive.

And then I get another thought. We *do* have a time machine. It's our scientific imagination. If we know how to read the rocks and minerals, the fossil claws and teeth and bones, we *can* travel back to the time of the raptor pack.